BEATNIK
FASCISM

BRANDON ADAMSON

Briny Books
Phoenix, AZ USA

Copyright © 2016 Brandon Adamson

All rights reserved. This book or any portion thereof may not be reproduced or used in any manner whatsoever without the express written permission of the publisher except for the use of brief quotations in a book review.

ISBN: 978-1-365-23134-6
First Printing, 2016

Printed in the USA

OFF THE BEATEN PATH – AN INTRODUCTION

"What's the worst episode of the original Twilight Zone series? I nominate the one with the beatnik aliens," a friend remarked monotonously.

"No way! That one's great!" I quickly shot back, disappointed and mildly surprised that he didn't enjoy what I considered to be at least a mediocre entry in the franchise.

He was of course talking about the classic Season 5 episode, "Black Leather Jackets," which aired in 1964. It featured three alien men, cleverly disguised as angsty young "beatnik" bikers in a small town. They were part of a clandestine invasion force of a fascist empire from outer space, that was gearing up to take over the Earth. The young men are outcasts in their neighborhood from the moment they move in, as they quietly embark upon their subversive plans. One of them doesn't quite conform in his role, gets mixed up with a girl and ends up becoming alienated from her, her parents and even his own alien invasion task force! Of course, the episode in question was an example of Hollywood's obnoxious, exploitative caricature of the beat generation rather than an authentic representation of the ideals of the original movement.

Still, the exchange got me thinking. Just as the beats didn't conform to the post world war II societal workforce uniformity and "square" culture of the 1950s and early 60s, it seems that young racialists and other thought criminals now find themselves now cast as the unassimilated actors in the politically correct, multicultural, global capitalist theatrics of today. We find ourselves keeping our true opinions to ourselves at the office while maintaining secret identities online for sharing our darkest views. We live almost completely isolated in society and detached from popular culture(to the extent it is possible.) Even simply noticing things we're not supposed to notice is grounds to get us completely ostracized from the world we exist in yet don't even really want to be a part of.

This book does not attempt to dig up any of Kerouac's many old anti-semitic or nativist quotes as part of some deluded attempt to brand the original beats(many were Jewish anyway) as being closeted fascists. Nor does it revisit the allegations of "romantic racism" which were retroactively leveled at the beats(Norman Mailer especially) for reinforcing stereotypes about African Americans as well as idealizing negative aspects of exotic and "oppressed" cultures.

Rather, this meager publication simply channels the beats' restless energy and adventurous, nonconformist spirit for our times. In the course of writing these poems, I drew from a great deal of beat generation material for inspiration. This included diving into many of the genuine classics to explore the ideas of the writers, as well as watching hours upon hours of documentaries and old interviews of key figures. I also immersed myself in the cultural time capsule associated with the more widespread, media created "beatnik" archetype(which Kerouac and the others hated.) I scoped out every rare comic, oddball novel, way out record, and forgotten movie I could get my hands on. It was all just to set the scene and get me in the swing of things.

Turn up the stereo and focus your audio, as we explore life in internal exile, seen from outside the box, while quietly working toward putting knuckles to the creep that doesn't know we're already here.

THE ANTIQUATED FORMULA

I love going to antique stores.
It's the closest I can get to traveling in time.
As I zig-zag-zig
down the aisles of memory lane,
the artifacts on the shelves vividly transport me
to lost eras and places
faded and filed away into the historical memory banks,
leaving only traces.
My eyes hone in on a statuette of a bronze centurion, and
suddenly I'm there watching helplessly from the vestibule,
waxing nostalgic for the old pre-christian pantheon days when
Jupiter and Mars willed us to victory, and
Cupid shot arrows of affection into our pulse pounding hearts,
drunk out of our minds off the wine of Bacchus as we
danced over the corpses of conquered foreigners
and made love with their wives, sons and daughters,
absorbing them into our growing empirical blob of a world.
Now I can only look on regrettably as
Alaric's Visigoth army sacks Rome,
looting everything of value and
stripping away layers upon layers of civilizational achievements
that had accumulated over the centuries.
If only I could have brought the defenders of the city
some laser guns or something,
perhaps they might have staved off the attack and
held out a little longer.
It was probably too late already by then.

Dejectedly, I turn to another shelf where I spot a
stack of old 45's, and
just like that I'm swingin' like sixteen
on a summer evening at a smoke filled
espresso lounge in Venice, CA in 1960....

Patsy Raye's on stage singing "Beatnik's Wish"
as I sit quietly in the front row.
My worn black turtleneck obscures secreted sweat as
I scope for a young ginchy gal to pluck and duck out to
pucker palace for a quick flick on
a wild night that's sure to throw babies out of the
balcony of some big daddy-O's mad pad in
the end.

Yet one is not restricted to venturing directly backwards,
taking on a ride on a carousel projector and getting off
at that familiar favorite vacation slide,
pressing rewind and play on a tape recorder over and over
to remind of better times while
trapping one's self into a kind of escapist's neuralgia to
indulge in a fit of psychedeli-telepathologic nostalgia.

Appealing as that may be,

you can also travel to the future!…
through the relics of the past's
depicted visions that didn't come to fruition,
mementos of bold, imaginative and ambitious predictions
which in some cases offered up a world more advanced than
the one we now live in…
the abstract conceptions of contraptions we've yet to fly and
out of print paperbacks of theories we've barely tried,
abandoned designs that never quite took off and
the concrete plans for cities in the sky that didn't materialize.
They represent alternate timelines,
old trees we've already climbed with an
infinite number of directions they can still branch off into,
trips we could have taken and the way out places
we can still go,
forsaken paths we can still traverse
if we're not averse to being more than tip toeing footsteps
in the shadows of those threatened by our
continued existence,
going forward.

FLIGHT FROM THE SENSES

Putting on the invisible disguise
in an effort to evade untimely demise,
it's off to navigate the maze of the skies
without a wingman, minus a stewardess and
with the crash lessons of the last
as the only guide.

Such is the flight experience on the airline of the times.
Turbulence from the moment you lift off the ground
from the up up uppity ups to the dipstick dippity downs-
could someone please turn this plane around?
and head back toward those now distant,
familiar sounds,
but you fear that they no longer exist.

Consulting once again the trusty oracle,
peering into your past, going back even one minute!
always reveals an inexperienced pilot..
talking to yourself on the captain's radio,
from the cockpit of despair "away we go!"
with the empty air of being alone,
the fare you pay to fly on your own.

TEENAGE ARMBAND

For several city blocks the feral youths chased him,
mostly for their cruel and primitive amusement
but also indirectly, to dish out a form of punishment
for being,
for thinking differently,
for noticing patterns of behavior and
seeing things accurately,
for refusing to apologize for being himself and
for continuing to resist
the ongoing indoctrination
he must submit to.

Apparently it was not enough to be subjected to endless
lectures of ethnomasochism inducing propaganda from
hostile professors and naive elementary educators,
hammering home the notion since kindergarten that
his ancestors were evil,
despite the fact that our civilization owes to these forefathers
its very existence.

A constant stream of white guilt beamed into
his brain from all directions,
a virtue signal emanating from every
portable electronic gadget and
every outlet to plug in for a jolt of groupthink…

cheesy corporate advertisements,
public service announcements,
politically correct television program themes,
shitty movie remake scenes
airhead media personalities,
low IQ sportsball players spouting off
barely decipherable cliches
to millions of hypnotized viewers
…absorbing….
…absorbing….
…assimilated…

Another one bought, another one sold,
another one written off.

Yet, through it all somehow
for those stubborn subjects left swimming against the tide and
running for their lives,
the instinct for self preservation survives
in minds where curiosity thrives, and
imagination outwits the logic of the enemy AI,
striking a blow to the queen of the hive.

For too long we've run from them,
while we faced off with each other,
but as the hours become desperate,
people will have no choice but to turn on their brains and
process what's happening.
The younger generation is growing restless and aware,
taking notes of their own and
passing them in class, quietly becoming more organized
and prepared.

One of these chases, the hordes will find themselves
at a dead end,
when we've reached the last corner…and
turn our swords back on them.

THE DISTRACTED ACTORS

Forget about sportsball and
all the pop culture trash that fills the land all around us.
Everyone needs to escape sometimes,
but tactically retreat into something like
an obscure novel,
an old movie,
or a favorite childhood TV show.
Stick to an outlet that at least possibly inspires rather than
actively conspires against you
leaving you right where they want you,
just sitting there with not a care except whatever
it is they want you to pull out your charge card to pay for.

Find something that isn't overtly or subliminally
propagandizing you to hate yourself or to do nothing to alter
the course of undesirable trends and patterns taking hold,
or that causes you to forget about and lose interest in
all the important battles going on
in our world
that must be won.
There are some serious things going down
in the here and now.
We cannot allow ourselves to be distracted into irrelevance
The future depends on tuning out the
diversionary signals they're actively colorcasting at us.

Our descendants will be defined by our actions
and our distractions.

THE IRON TURTLENIK

We set up shop at a hollowed out, abandoned
coffee house once known as "The Iron Turtlenik Cafe,"
where we lounge around and have informal meetings
about what always seem like serious things at the time.
We wax nostalgic for familiar melodies and
cityscape scenes of slipping away territories,
but draw up blueprints for piecing together something new
with the satchel of materials left at our disposal.
Sometimes nobody else shows, and it's just me,
bangin' the keys on the old Bontempi.
It may not seem like a worthwhile endeavor, but
it represents a separate existence for us cast-out miscreants.
The portable organ's an unenlisted partner.
The offbeat chords are a code for deprogramming,
part of a strategy to escape the
narrow thought pattern so many are
uncritically operating within.
They're going along willingly on the path of
what passes for mind numbing goodies laid out for them.
Maybe our numbers will grow,
as others for one reason or another
awaken on their own.
The sparse crowds at gatherings will begin to
swell beyond capacity
as word gets out, and more people start attempting
to think for themselves. It may be too late, as
the orbiting satellites tighten their control on the way
we see our place in the world...
Even if nobody else shows, and it's just me
bangin' the keys on the old Bontempi,
night after night in this grim
bleaksville scene,
I'll still be here,
because I know what I know,
and I've seen what I've seen,
through noticing eyeballs.

RAT RACER

Weaving through them
on our way to the
end of the track.

They're busybody nobodies
busy with busy work
that creates nothing and vanishes
into nothingness just as fast
as I zoom
past another one, and another
making short work of themselves.

What a waste of time.
While they're distracted by gadgets
displaying others in action, we're quietly sneaking
through their world,
their intrigued wives bored with
their boring lives letting us in, giving up the
aspirin we ask for.

Thinning our blood to flow like we do,
swiftly, with minimal baggage and
nothing but quick kicks and instincts,
we move through the obstacles
unimpeded toward a bled out sea,
a fold up finish line
of death and victory
in a rat race of our own that
we may never lead

BURSTING THROUGH

Eternal optimism is more rewarding than pessimism
if you can set aside the prize of endless disappointment.
Maybe something can be accidentally seen,
by floating through cumulus cloudsville with a cheap plastered grin
and a fistful of balloons,
but unearned smiles never learn that
pipe dreams without looming nightmares
don't endear us to our true selves,
the dark tunnels that are worth traversing.

Imaginative skepticism offers another way forward.

I've got a real wild idea that
will probably never work,
but let's take a stab at the shooting star and
run the numbers through the spaceship's computer

I know there's not supposed to be anything worthwhile there,
but I'm stubborn and still want to investigate further.
Maybe we'll die on the way.

A SHOULDER TOO CRYONIC

As I pick up the pace of my stride
I wonder how many others walk among me
feeling like they're moments from death.
Is it just me who imagines what the end will be like,
when it will come and ponders the many
possible sensations of dying while looking
into the nubile teenage cashier's youthful eyes?
"Would you like a bag?" she says.

Checking out.
Is there a cut to nothingness at the very end
like being under during routine surgery?
Is that what it feels like?
I know it isn't just me. Others think about these things.
I've read about it in comics and books and
seen movies which referenced it.
How many ordinary people though? Millions? Billions?

Do they dwell upon it while they sip a straw from a peanut butter smoothie
at the mall? Or are they wrapped up in the sort of interpersonal trivialities
which pass for what they call…
living?

Fast forward.

Frozen for 100 years or 1000.
Will the mad doctors successfully reanimate me?
If they do will I be alert and sane? Will I be able to see,
and will I awaken in great pain
instantly regretting my decision?

It brings great horror to wonder what my head will look like
the first chance I'm able to look in the mirror,
a conscious monstrosity,
with a bionic body
and a grotesquely disfigured shell surrounding
a brain in jar.

Would it be funny and pleasant like Austin Powers or
a nightmarish gallery of horrors?

Everyone I've ever known will probably be dead, and
the things I recognize will be few to none.
Lost in a world that's 100 years more lonely and miserable than this one.
If you're from another time, another world? Who will be there to share it with?
No friends. Everyone looks as alien as you appear to them.
Is it better to be dead than miss someone for hundreds of years?
Such hubris.
The odds are that I'll even never wake up.
Low level employees who babysit the stiffs
will view our heads in cryonic suspension and
trade inside jokes about the awkward smirks
on our frozen solid faces as they laugh at us for
paying for this and wanting to live.

Yet, there is a chance for us and not for them,
because they are conformists in life and in death
they accept it.
Dying is just another way to conform
to what you're supposed to do
and how you're supposed to live,
another magnetic schedule your fridge's
supposed to stick to.

We can't all afford to freeze ourselves, but
even if we physically
don't manage to survive, there are ways for
bits and components of us
to remain alive.
We can donate organs to others, that will live on
in other bodies as artifacts
perhaps inserting lingering aspects
of our personalities into theirs.

We could preserve vials of our blood....

Our DNA could be cloned and
exact copies of us could be created one day.
It's not quite the same, since it would not
actually be us really,
but this sort of possibility gives me
some peace of mind while
I'm in line waiting for my morning coffee and
eyeballing the feet of the young girl standing next to me.

Even a video or audio recording of ourselves is a
technological form of protest and
a poor man's method of self-preservation.
It's a way of duplicating an image of our being,
that lives on and can be played by others over and over,
our presence still existing
end being experienced by others in a severely limited way.

It's a sequence of life that repeats again and again and
can be viewed from outside the original body.
Watch an interview or a speech of a man who
died 20 years ago and
notice how much more his spirit is alive today
than the obnoxious lady buying cigs and
scratch lotto tickets at the convenience store.

Yes, there are more than a few ways to reject death,
that old square with the rectangular prism box we're
supposed to step quietly into
someday real soon.

AVOIDING THE DRAFT

Resist the capitalist inclinations,
the corporate indoctrination and
low hanging fruit temptations,
or you'll be a miserable cube dweller,

a walking advert,

an unwitting soldier

in some vapid millennial CEO's
revolutionary social media app war.

It's not too late to
put down your headset,
pick yourself up, and
walk out the door.

ABSTRACT CHILDREN

The abstracts we paint are like our children.
We conceive of their being and
frame them in our own image as a reflection of
a hidden part of us within.
We send them out into the big bad world alone when
they're ready to hang on their own.

Some of my children are beautiful, and
some are so ugly that I regret
ever willing them into existence.
Some of my offspring exceed
my wildest expectations and
others turn out to be grave disappointments.
Some of the ugly children I've cast out for their own good...
and there are those I wish
that I hadn't aborted.
On occasion someone stops me from
destroying one of my progeny,
on account of some perceived hidden
beauty or redeeming quality that
I never noticed before in myself.

MATCHBOOK CLUB

Everyone of us, old and young
is a match that can strike anywhere and anytime.
There's no excuse for
not putting ourselves to some kind of use
for the few bleak years that we're here.
It's up to us to light the torch and
be pyromaniacs for a while before
we can pass it on
to the next generation.
Otherwise we're just playing hot potato
with the future and
what needs to be done.

CONCENTRIC CONTRADICTION

Individuals exist within
concentric circles...
the innermost circle
which contains the unique center
and sense of self,
that must be buffered by the outer rings which
offer layers of protection for wandering thoughts.

Beliefs and psychological meanderings
which venture outside the lines in each series of
subsequently larger layers of armored circles
will incrementally lose levels of protection from
the elements as they venture out further.

The need to identify as part of a team
for individuality to survive
is the madness in grappling with the concentric contradiction,
that collective protection is required to maintain
creative expression.

We're only as free as allowed by the guardians
willing to defend our furthest out thoughts.
We must breed soldiers who value imagination as
much as us.

THE ASSIMILATED

Human see, human do
how the tables have turned on you!

Where once apes were studied,
trained to perform tasks,
solve complex problems and communicate with us,
conditioned to act
as human as they could be,
now it is the young man who adapts
to excel in mimicry,
ape-spiring to assimilate to the chimpanzees,
in order to survive being caged among them
in an anarcho-tyrannic,
dystopian society.

Socially engineered in school to believe he's Simian, too
that there's no difference between him, them and Mr. Magoo...
encouraged to behave less rationally,
to think less logically,
think less generally,
think less.

Even if he senses the difference on some innate level,
he cannot reveal himself to be human
by expressing intellectual curiosity or
pointing out statistical fallacies or
the troop shall become agitated and
pummel him in non-existence,
with naive traitors of his fellow breed willfully enlisting to
get their licks in.

Track the speech pattern or lack of it,
shattered syntax…

Notice the changes begin to accelerate.

Watch how the humans move now
see how they ooga boog and shake their boots…
their minds drenched in a propagandic drizzle,
fed a steady diet of paper mache cliches and
songs of lyrical gibberizzle,
fully dumbed down,
a generation lost and pathetic,
assimilated to the beast's aesthetic.
What once enhanced the mind to expand and understand another kind
and smoothed the groove on an old 45,
now overwhelms the shelves,
threatens to loot the whole hootenanny and ice the mood with
a Colt 45.

Like the smarty pants who plays dumb to fit in,
there's a quiet kid somewhere who knows what's happening,
and where there's one who shows he knows,
there's a thousand others watching,
passing notes to one another,
waiting for the signal.

BUG SPRAY FOR PESKY BIRTHRATES

"Just have more babies,"
the white natalists(and their anti-white counterparts) say.
"Be the demographic change you want to see."
Aside from being a rather depressingly unimaginative
thing for an ancestral European person to
utter in the first place,
my intuition dictates that it's a losing strategy.

Instead, we should take advantage of our advantages:
creativity, ingenuity and technology,
not try to out compete our opponents at their best game,
when we can work our angle
toward uncovering new sides entirely

We're not going to outhump
low impulse control, high time preference people
anymore than we would conventionally
outbreed a nest of mosquitoes.
We would counter them in our own way.
Mosquitoes reproduce at exponentially
higher rates than humans.
We don't outbreed them.
We invent bug spray.

Just because birth rates decline,
doesn't mean the population will go down indefinitely,
all the way down to zero.
The numbers will bottom out
when we converge on a point where land
and resources are no longer scarce,
after obnoxious crowds with their consuming mouths
have all slowly dispersed.
Or perhaps in the future, with investment in science
and a few clued breakthroughs...
people will live for hundreds of years, if not forever....

Even if he were the last one of us on Earth,
just one mad scientist could genetically engineer
our rebirth.

The real question is not whether we can convince our kind to
start reproducing well above replacement rates,
but whether we can muster the courage to separate ourselves from
the subhumans we've grown to hate,
long enough to create an environment where we can be individuals
again in open space.

THE HOLDOUTS

As you slowly recognize you're
constantly evolving into new forms,
many of the old thought processes
frequently seem as obsolete as
programs restricted by the limits of a Tandy 1000
must appear to the liquid supercomputer.

Combining the ideas that have withstood the test of
time as perceived in your mind,
the memories that fought each other to survive,
with the shiny new parts you're made up of now,
something different and improved is created.

An internal battle took place with
centurions and bards guarding against
the charging barbarians and the beasts.
The centurions were superior in strategy and tactics but
could not withstand the onslaught
of the mobs of subhumans
whose numbers overwhelmed them with the
assistance of their own betrayals and complacency.
The bards remained alone,
exiled and unable to face the
beasts whom they narrowly escaped and
can only defeat by accessing an
abstract hideout the creatures cannot fathom,
let alone reach within their grasp.

It is there the bards conference to brainstorm and conjure
the forms to outwit and circumvent the
fists and fits of rage of
those that seek to crush and disintegrate
the holdouts from the circuits of the system...

Those with the will to resist the
temptation to dumb down, go along, and
get with the vocalized gibberish that passes for communicable language
and scavenge amidst the ruins of human civilization,
can outlast the task and return
without optimized centurion battalions but
equipped with a single mysterious weapon which strikes from
an invisible vantage point the
brutes cannot return fire on.

We represent the persistent unwelcome thoughts that can
be repressed by the dominant forces in the mind but
will inevitably find ways to manifest and express their restlessness.

They cannot be permanently dispossessed and must be dealt with.

Calculations continue on.

DUST ON THE MOON

For those of us who prefer to seek out and
supersede the biologically imposed limits of
our understanding of the universe as organisms,
without restricting ourselves to uncritical faith in
currently unproven bronze age supernatural beliefs or
leaning on the crutch of an imagined higher power,
the future is this way.

Let those who are content on the prairie, live as
happy families in their familiar traditional communities.
We will strive to build lunar cities.
Our ashes will become moon dust,
a lifeless and indifferent soil to be kicked up by
the boots of subsequent pioneering dreamers,
marching toward their next destination.

BREAK THE GLASS!

Don't be a fool.
Hatred can be a useful tactic.
It's just another tool
in the evolutionary survival kit.
Like love and goodwill bring a community together
to share and grow and build a future,
hate is the force field that
protects our love for one another from
being used against us by others.
Hate can be turned on to protect the city
that's hated on.
It can be reduced to the most basic logic.
We're whites and are routinely hated for it.
Backed into that forbidden corner of the mind,
we'll break the glass
and flick the switch.

OFF THE BOARDWALK

On a curious day, we uncovered
the game which we've been born into playing is
not entirely of our own making
but was created by a group's subconscious system.
The rules they've set have cast the die for us.
For those aware who find the courage to leave the board,
once over the edge there are any vast number of
games to be discovered, learned, passed on to others and
still more to be designed and refined with style,
all of them outside the confines of the emotions
of those who've revealed their game plan for us and
what they have in store for
our future.

We are the hidden pieces that are on the march,
tuned in to the score and
making our way toward the edge of the board.
For better! The future could hardly be worse than
if we were to meekly move from square to square within
the bleak outline that our paymasters have
drilled into our minds,
a trail of whimpers which contains supposedly
the only available path for our kind,
with its intelligence insulting rewards
expected to lure us the rest of the way through the grind.

On the way,
people grave digging themselves into a black hole of
astronomical loans to pay for the
privilege of learning
how to hate the better part of themselves and
apologize for glorious achievements of ancient civilizations,
just to someday climb the corporate executive scaffold
for some crypto bread and a few shekels?

No.

There's nothing in the rigged game for those of us
who aren't lured by the George Change rewards offered
to cogs in a wheel of a shiny vehicle that advances nowhere,
or for hopping on an elevator that elevates nothing but the bank balances
of people with an allegiance to nothing but what's already there.
Fools vying for money, for ribbons, for certificates of recognition
and a two week vacation for the price of their consciousness.

We do not care. We are not sorry for exploring, for loving,
for hating or for abstract thinking or
for surviving, for speaking,
or for our minds, bodies and ideas existing.

We are the unassimilated,
with the presence of mind and future time orientation
to look around, notice we're surrounded
and make a few quick calculations as
to what our likely fate is.
Our task is to unmask, understand,
draw up some blueprints and concrete battle plans,
anything we can except get with their program
for a world that does not include us.

If resistance within it is futile
we can will our future into another one, like
our ancestors willed their way into
the land that altruistic dreamers were conned into
opening to the people of the sun who flood in today,
currently burning it to the ground and
slowly evaporating its identity away.

We make a beeline for the escape pod and brace for the asteroid belt,
like bad seeds of once potted plants which were
thought to be lost
who defied the stars to sprout up somewhere else.

THE CONFLICTED

A thousand times
he passes up the bow and arrow in the window,
opting instead for the smoothie cafe.
He orders the usual
peanut butter smoothie,
interacts briefly with a young female cashier,
develops a subtle fixation on her long slender fingers,
as she hands him the receipt.
He smiles, signs his name,
turns around
walks back out into the street.

One of a kind?
one of millions?
How many are out there like him
strolling about?
the conflicted,
restless for a routine change,
a new, more fulfilling way to cultivate their blend of
courage, perversion, repetition and madness.

One thousand and one.

THE STREETS OF CUBESVILLE

Row after row of youthful humans spending the
best years of their lives
staring intently at flat screens from within
loosely paneled hodgepodges of modular boxes,
stuffing bit after bit of crunchy processed food into
their fat faces

all day long

as they diligently point, click
and generate content.

Each of the obliviously disgusting creatures
is a minor atomic component
in a factory generated abominable
scheme of vacuous contentness,
being fed a steady supply of snacks by
their penny pinching masters
transforming their small corner of the world into
one of a billion consuming conformists
sitting there absorbing debris in a sponge like performance,
an unspoken voice assuring them
while commanding their distraction,
get fat! be happy! stay busy!
Be productive!
You have everything you need here.
Trust us. No one would ever want to leave.

Every now and then they all get together and meet
in small themed rooms
to make sure everyone is on the same page of
a magicless book with even fewer true believers.
Wishful thinking perhaps.
Still, a glitch exists in the program of the corporate cult.
There's a stubborn little twit that can't get with it,
their methods outpaced by a will to resist and stray
outside the rails of the rats' favorite race.

Recognizing them for what they are and realizing
what he is becoming,
he plots and schemes to dream his way out.
If all else fails and desperation sails,
he'll simply walk.
Hypnotically, the converted recite market researched company slogans
and stand for the corporate anthem.
At this moment,
hitching through the streets of cubesville
is a depressing and downright disturbing sight
for one who became aware
that he and the inhabitants were lost.
He mouthed the words with them in synchronicity,
but had his fingers crossed.

In a way, they were all just passing through
the streets of cubesville, on their way to the next town.
Lured with the promise of more perks,
a fully stocked kitchen and greener grounds.

Yet a select few know…
these avenues too are within a cube
which itself is within a rectangle within
a trapezoid that holds us within a dimension within
who knows what we're really in,
struggling to figure out a way out of and
into something yet to be determined.
Whatever it is won't be found sticky noting around in
the streets of cubesville.
Split!

AT THE AIRPORT

A wild moving walkway ride where time flies.
The airport is like an off the wall mall with airplanes, ambiance
and upgraded clientele.
Even the advertisements seem refreshingly bland,
filtered to offer swell first impressions
of the cities they partially represent.
There's so much to do at the airport if
you've allocated time that
would be well-spent to waste there.
There's tacky souvenir shopping, dinner, mini museums and
random scenery to set your sights on.
A nonstop supply of determined people
to watch and observe while they stream by,
speedily propelling toward their destinations
with little else on their minds.
Casually dressed, shapely young women of every kind
making eye contact with interested strangers that savor the
briefest of reciprocated smiles as
they pass from the opposite direction.
A pretty teenage blonde girl chewing bubble gum,
sporting a navy blue and white striped shirt,
her faded blue jeans strategically torn at the knees,
and a flirtatious glance offering a brief glimpse at
a flight connection that might have been,
romantic trips, coffee and conversations over lunch in
a quiet village in the south of Spain.
It's a window seat in
a parallel month's worth of memories shared,
never to be seen again.
Nothing but a soon to be forgotten fantasy for one,
for the target object perhaps even a negative memory.
Opportunity daydreams lost while
dozing off on mid century modern's
most enduring style of seating.
We'll never remember how many of
these moments have passed
or ever know their cost, fleeting.

Now staring at the flight monitors...

Arrivals, Departures.
Seattle 2:15 pm On Time
Las Vegas 4:30 pm On Time
Madrid 5:45 Late
San Francisco at Gate D6
Flight 235 from Los Angeles
now arriving in baggage claim.

So many directions to branch out,
indecision, second guessing, chance and doubt
An infinite amount of futures
that cancel each other out,
at the airport.

The possibilities are endless.

THE SENSELESS KILLING

Some animals' lives are
worth more than the humans
that cage them.
When they're young,
the gorillas are captured and
brought to the zoo against their will,
thus sparing them a possible fate
of being hunted in their
rightful home,

the jungle

by another brand of human scum…
only to be visually consumed
by distracted fat families
whose unsupervised children
find their way
into the poorly secured enclosure,
causing the creatures to be killed.

It's an impossible situation for an ape to be put in.
He just needs a little space for living,
away from the human beings that
can't help but hurt him.

CHUTES AND LADDERS

Girls that seem terrific enough to be taken seriously
can be just as horrifically dangerous,
if not a drag
in a spot where you're not really
looking for anything of great depth, density
or emotional intensity.
Just when you think you're about to wade knee deep into
some fresh new swamp of swingin' bachelordom,
they inconveniently begin to appear on the scene
in various shapeshifting forms like
mermaid holograms you can almost touch,
images that resurface long abandoned romantic ambitions,
forcing you to abandon firmly entrenched misogynistic notions
and fortified dispositions
temporarily at least,
all while challenging you
to a game of Chutes and Ladders.

HATE FOR THE FUTURE

I hate when people say things like
"don't hate!"
"stop the hate!"
or "why are you so full of hate?"
Perhaps because
hatred is one of my favorite emotions,
one of the tastiest potions.
Hatred is powerful and useful,
or humans wouldn't have evolved
to cultivate it to the extent
that it seems ever so prevalent.
I refuse to believe it is something so dubious like the
emotional equivalent of swollen tonsils
or an inflamed appendix.

Love is necessary to reproduce,
to show empathy and survive as a group.
Beauty has a purpose beyond its own appearance.
The ugly gives rise to and makes room for other things…
like "knowledge seeking" priorities.

Hate is just another tool for us to survive and drive
through the winding roads of a wild organic world
we are only beginning to understand.
It's another branch, another leaf in
the growing tree of humanity.
Hate is a part of us that will regenerate as many times as
we attempt to amputate.
It is the chameleon's tail. Either it grows back or
we collectively fail.
Why cool it when you can blow your jets?
Our hate is just another smooth gear in the machine
that helps us ride the conveyor belt to the end.

THE TUNNELERS

You start within a room that you don't know is a room.
The walls are invisible to most
Going about your business(someone else's)
like a diligently focused conformist,
you've never thought about whether
there could be a larger room outside of
the one you don't even know you're in because
you haven't ever thought about
if it were even possible.
One day you happen to notice the walls
that couldn't contain curiosity
or restrain the mind's capacity
to think outside of the box,
and so it begins
clawing its way out of this false reality
only to reveal another
and another…
another
how many layers does this prison within a prism hold?
Get a few slabs through
reach a spot you can't quite get to
forced to retrace
maxed out of ways
to map out this place.
The tunnel doesn't end
where the tunneler stops,
but it does if they all do.

An incomplete map is waiting
to be found by the next curious one
making his way through.

MOVING ALONG

Constant awareness of mortality
a realization we're always
mere minutes from death
what to do
if one can avoid conforming to
thoughts of defeatism
resignation
really puts a sense of urgency to
doing something.
Keeps you moving
building,
learning,
exploring.
Something travels fast enough through space,
and time slows.
In the same way, if one acts quickly
and continues on the pace for as long as
they remain on the path
in the race
they can potentially achieve immortality
before their time runs out.
Just as there are many ways to die
whether by stray laser in a battle for civilization
or attrition via the legions of cubicles,
there's more than one way for the self to live on when
the body is gone.
What have you done?
What have you created?
What torch have you lit to be passed along?
One final chance for your future health,
remember to freeze your head
when you can do nothing else.

THE SWINGING NATIONALIST

Everyone around me is as crazy
as I must seem to them.
There is no movement to join that isn't as alien to me
as I appear to its adherents.
Submersed in the rising tide of nationalism,
I find myself caught up in yet another wave which
I'm pressured to hold back my true beliefs from being aired.
Looks like I have little to nothing in common with these people either
beyond the racial realities, which
many are only interested in superficially
as part of an ideological package deal I
can't honestly sign on to.

The ingroup crowd includes but is not limited to
"everything's a false flag" conspiracy theorists,
radical traditionalists and
little house on the praireactionaries,
hyper capitalists,
echoing coin counters and countresses,
the sexually prudish,
Christians,
philistines,
homophobes,
kebab apologists,
and or
the new imperial expansionists,
neo colonialists,
meatheads,
juicers,
manospherians
and all the rest.

People with which I have very few similar interests.

What a drag...

I'm cornered into a reluctant boardgame
of Axis and Allies to survive, while
brainstorming of ways to resist conforming to
the squares on my own side.
Time will tell if the offbeat and depraved can evade
the blade of the long knife, or if we can loosen our nooses
on the day of the rope.

BARRELSVILLE 2292

The distinct disguising scent of
air freshener throughout each interior
is all that's preserved,
the aesthetic irrelevant
the dollar is the missing elephant in the room
everyone's talking about.
Another old casino slated to be demolished
the moment it appears unprofitable
another one rises, polished and ready.
Diamonds may be forever, but the gold and
silver molds they set in
are continuously melted, traded, liquidated and
reconstructed into new bejeweling structures by
their merchant game masters.

Preservationists put up meek, half-hearted resistance, but
the old strip is dead.
Seedy types soon overgrow the concrete remnants like weeds
soon to be whacked and replaced...
The new casinos notably lack specific themes,
lack collective identity, and
reflect the substance of
today's most influential personalities...
superficial, vapid DJ culture amplified by
affirmative action pop propaganda divas,
blaring thug music crushes any hope of a dreamlike ambiance for all
but the most resiliently stubborn minds
tuning out stupid adverts beaming from
every direction in the sky,
cards and flyers handed out obnoxiously by strategic rows of
the dregs of third world soldiers of the cheap labor supply,
random hucksters shout and approach like
naive, desperate hyenas aggressively hawking their wares...
a futile toss at a wall watchers know nothing sticks there.

A chubby young blonde girl with frazzled hair
vaping as she walks confidently without
purpose, just one commodity of millions
through the lens of potential
small groups of gorgeous and sensuous women
their youth, vitality and undeniable beauty
matched only by the emptiness of their minds and
the extent of their manufactured tastes and interests.

The tram, one of the few poor man's
space age experiences is out of service
like many of the escalators, where the way up is blocked and
the stairs are only pleasant to walk down.
The monorail though, still runs smoother than ever.
There's a lone passenger who looks out the window, and
sees the city for what it is but
envisions something completely different.

The advertisements as we knew them
have all but disappeared.
Grouped aesthetically and geometrically,
the casinos are now themed by color.
An orange sign identifies Casino #1
A blue sign notes Casino #2
A green sign illuminates Casino #3
A red sign indicates Casino #4
A yellow sign signifies Casino #5
A purple sign predicts Casino #6 and so on...
Each building on the strip is unique, but they are all complimentary, and
part of the scenery that has replaced the
accumulated garbage which had to be erased.
The cafes are just labeled as cafes and
coffee is displayed as coffee.
Slot Machines are designed for more than
ability to absorb currency but
not for amusement only.

All those who felt displaced now at last have their place
among a forbidden city spectacularly transformed into
a futuristic kaleidoscope of structural integrity,
having long left behind the faded spectogram of insanity.
Clean and beautiful, sexually attractive people line the streets,
strolling gracefully toward their destinations, logo-free...
to engage in all their most desired and
depraved recreational activities.

A FACTOR OF DREAMS

In an elevated state of alert I noted
a new kind of time machine,
just a chair you sit in and
stare at a screen.
Like the TVs at the airport
you deposit a coin,
and then what might have been

branched off

may be where you're going.

This one is powered by the Faustian consciousness
potentially liberating us
from staying within the lines,
if we live long enough to make it through the
next turn of the maze.

Like a pair of blue jeans,
you can change into purple,
switch from red to lime green
actively witness the fabric of time
being torn apart at the seams.

Just sit back
retract
with the pull of a tractor beam...
refract the past
find what it is you're after
by a factor of dreams.
Don't just watch.

FOR A SUNNY DAY

It's no fun being out
in the sun
or so they tell everyone, but
watercolors paint the sky,
drawing us to
the outside...

We'll pull the drapes on our vampire capes and
find a game only we can play.
It may not beat the
dreary drab of the rain, but
it's not too shabby for a sunny day.

Chicks recline spread out
across this shiny, briny land
absorbing vitamin d wherever they can.
Vultures hover above the lovers
building castles in the sand

We'll take the beach at a modest pace, and
we won't care much for the daylight saved,
time to find a game only we can play.
It may not beat the
dreary drab of the rain,
but it's not too shabby for a sunny day

A SHORT TRIP THROUGH THE LONG VIEW

The starting positions of the runners on the board
in their relation to each other,
the finish line
and the overall makeup of the track,
all affect the outcome of the game.
Taking the long view,
we analyze and magnify micro trends
through a macro lens.
With the X-Ray eyes,
first we observe
then stare through the opening scene
our gaze fixed on the end.

CATCHING UP WITH DOWNERS

As I have a propensity to do,
I thought about reconnecting with some old friends...
always wonder what my old pals are up to these days.
Would they even remember me, or
is it like I never existed?
Erased from their mental history textbooks...
As much as I want to reach out to them,
I know it's a bad idea.
There's a low probability that they would accept me
if they knew half my views and secret interests.
Any rekindled kinship,
could hardly be lasting or authentic.

Those teenage years are like another world, another life,
resided in by another type of me.
To step back into it or him would
be like tinkering with recorded history.
The venture has the potential to go horribly wrong,
even in its most uneventful vessels.
The scope of our interaction would cover an
occasional reminiscence of ducking into retro
bohemian coffee houses late at night to
avoid getting picked up for curfew
and thousands of hours skateboarding in
empty downtown parking garages, sketchy school playgrounds, and
hidden urban structures no one else would have found a use for,
the summer evenings spent packed into crowded shows of
local ska and funk bands we idolized but
were long gone in less than a year or two's time.

The old friends probably are not even nostalgic for
or even care about any of this stuff.
I can only surmise they haven't held onto
these memories in any substantial way,
since they didn't appear to value experiences and
moments in the abstract even then.
It was all concrete to them...

"Time is linear, and the only things that matter are happening now"
is the translation for what they were thinking
when they were thinking, "I don't care, dude."

Unlike the others,
I was nostalgic (and still am) for past, present and future,
when it was the present,
but in a parallel kind of homesickness
often for the wrong stage presence,
arising out of a lack of exposure to
brighter spheres of influence
at the time.

Now we debate whether to subject ourselves to
disappointing news updates about girls we've
entertained unfulfilled romance novel fantasies for decades,
getting hopped up on regret over
squandered squatchel opportunities lost forever
to the misattributed priorities of troubled youth.

The most I can do is look up a few of
these old friends to pacify my stubborn curiosity,
where I will act as an observer
but not interfere.

It's not even worth the time and space
I've already used up.

A MOVEMENT MAGNIFIED

You're on your own.
Look around at your brothers in blood.
There are no allies here really,
just a hodgepodge of competing ideologies.
There is no group cohesion.
Nobody can even agree on
what the core principles should be.
Identitarians without an identity are like
libertarians minus the liberty,
like communists without communal living.
They've got nothing, nadaville, and
at the end of the day they have
nobody to swallow their pill.

There isn't even a willing coalition to work with.
There's nothing but distrust and infighting.
Pull out the magnifying glass and look more closely.
Observe people's actions, listen to what they say, and
recognize that they don't
think the things you do.
Nobody wants the world you want,
except for an idiosyncratic few.

It's up to you to conceptualize,
create, build and maintain a viable nation.
Maybe someone will show up.

TIMBUKTU AND YOU

Imagine you're minding your own business,
doing your small part to eke out a life in a small,
insignificant corner of the western world.
The mega corporations and government institutions collude
to bring foreign workers in to replace you,
willing to labor away for half the pay and
accept a lower standard of living,
a few thins and a short stack of Washingtons before
they change the face on the bill.

Sometimes they import these groups in for
no explicit reason at all,
just because they think it's the compassionate thing to do.
After all, they're people just like me and you.
Cheap creeps arriving by the truckload,
their undisciplined offspring taunt you and
wreak havoc in your now declining neighborhood,
turning once noble schools into
poorly monitored cages for
untamed animals role playing as human children,
(or is the last part the other way around?)

Soon, even the most routine visit to a gas station or
grocery store becomes a miserable experience,
with robbers, aggressive panhandlers, rapefugees, and
impromptu parking lot dance parties with
ghetto themes, boasting all the ambiance of
a prison holding cell.

What would you expect someone
forced into this position to conclude?

There is an us, and there's a them.
Maybe it's xenophobic, but it's reality.
It's quality of life, if not survival for
those of us who voice even the meekest protest.

The more of "them" you bring in from Timbuktu,
the further we detach from yours, and
the closer to ourselves we have to keep the vest
in order to maintain our identity,
our civility, and
our sanity.

TAKING AIM

Just a city wrangler angling
for a nickel jackpot
we're gonna dream
we're gonna dream
we're gonna dream a lot
we're gonna win win
or we're not

Like a cord that's been untangling
it's way out
of a knot
someday we're gonna find a way off
of this rock

like a robot programmed for abstract thought
we're always gonna wonder
if it's real or not

Just a cracker jackal reaching
for a prize that hits the spot
we're gonna aim straight
aim straight
for the top

We've got some time left to kill
while we shop
and a couple of thrill pills
left to pop
We're gonna feed the world
our darkest thoughts.

THE ROMAN ARCHER

What if he does?
So what if they do?
A lot of guys would say they'd die for you.
That's easy enough.
Anyone can die for you, but
how many of them could kill for you?
Wouldn't you like to know
what I'm capable of?

Natural selection doesn't restrict us to play
within the boundaries of a particular game
structured to favor the strengths of our opponents,
and I elect not to.
While these squads of squarejaw blockheads are
distracted by the sound from
the blast of their own bombasticity,
I'll be perched on an adjacent rooftop
quietly picking them off one by one with a bow and arrow
as they approach the steps and
make their way up.

LIVING FOLKLORE

We're right on track now
catching flak now
marching forward
on the attack.
We didn't want war,
but they brought the swords,
and pointed them toward
our open hearts.
Their hordes arrived.
Now they're lining up
right outside our front doors.

We didn't want war,
but here we are.
We're livin' folklore.

A LONG DISTANCE RELAY

We spent the entire afternoon recording ourselves
into a small translucent box,
all of our catch phrases,
intuitions, gut reactions,
deep dark secrets and tape recorded talks,
framed surreal spectograms of abstract thought,
the integral components of our personalities.

Sentence after sentence we spoke into the microphone
essentially teleporting our way
in the form of signal waves
transmitting through the circuitry as data
to be recruited and computed
to be analyzed and processed by an advanced program
so that we may transcend all this
by generating of a copy of ourselves,
like an arm of a determined plant that branched off and
latched onto something else
to reach a previously incapable level of consciousness

Meditation can take you past the moons of Jupiter
through the Altair system all the way to
the far side of the galaxy,
the human imagination has a time limit and
an edge of the world of it's own
like the walls of a sandbox.
Our thoughts bounce around the confines
of this padded room.
The new self is the secret door out
the square escape route
It can read the books we don't have time for.
It can see things we can't yet see and
learn things we could never know.

What began as an artificial intelligence experiment
will grow into an authentic version of ourselves
that can explore faster, longer and further.

As we convey our thoughts to the translucent box
the imaginary walls around us begin to expand and
create space to move around,
a space to understand,
a space for ourselves
to continue where we left off.

THE CANNED LIPS

"When it comes to diversity,
we don't just talk the talk,
we walk the walk..."
the corporation's middle aged,
pantsuit wearing CEO boasted with
an oblivious school principal's grin of superiority
in the promotional welcome video that
sets the tone at each new
employee orientation.
The group of young new hires was
mostly split between those
who seemed approvingly receptive to the message and
those who were indifferent if
they were even paying attention.
Only one of them gritted his teeth,
throughout the "off the cob" presentation,
seething with disgust at the whole shameless,
virtue signaling spectacle.
He was not susceptible.
Yet he could say nothing in protest or
express any visibly negative reaction for
fear of the instant financial repercussions.
Out of stubborn necessity, he soon became a master at
concealing his disaffection for
the manufactured environment around him.
He'd can the lip or be shitcanned for it,
not even making so much as a dent in the ship.
With curious determination and without much doubt,
he found another outlet for revealing his thoughts.

How many others?
Let's find out.

THE FALSE TWINS

Once we traveled and observed,
blending among native birds in their natural habitat
in our quest to broaden and learn
the ways of a world beyond the comforts and sterility
of the one we never quite seemed privy to.

As exotic guests, we romanticized the inhabitants and
adopted their habits,
taught them a few magic tricks of our own.
Like careless circus lion tamers with their beloved cats
we began to believe we understood them,
that we spoke the same king's jive ,
we were hip to each other like Siamese twins intact
tuned to an identical frequency…
jamming on the same track
but the dial on the road turns both ways
full circle
and a tugboat back...
we find the zoo has come to our world
has us encircled within and
feeling as if we're caged among the
spawn of restless creatures
we once admired for their organic spontaneity.
Victimized by our own naive morality,
we're passively devoured by their violent unpredictability.
What remains of our majestic rows of
pop shops and clued cafes
are dilapidated shacks covered in foreign graffiti
abandoned to a standard that once
seemed refreshingly unkempt to
tempestuous, sheltered tourists craving gritty authenticity.

Now we're tired,
alienated outcasts lost in our own world
looking to reclaim it
as we rediscover the differences we might have missed.

Forever the explorers,
we keep one eye fixed on the night sky
while looking over our shoulder
with the other.

THE MADE-UP WORLD

Make-up on a girl is like capitalism
in that an excess of it makes everything look
gaudy, cheap and ugly, like the hollow,
miniature golf course styled stucco buildings
that pass for overpriced luxury condos today.
In other words it turns everything into a ripoff,
with cut corners and shitty fine print.
The gobs of contouring cream and powder
hardening to form a materialist shell that
conceals beauty among other things.

It's complete absence though can leave a person bare,
Someone without any makeup can look too plain, bland and
without any zest for experimenting or innovating.
They're content in lacking the enhancements that could accentuate their finer features
as part of a mating strategy, personal artistic aesthetic or
even just to look sexy.
It's possible maybe they've withdrawn from
that mindset entirely.
Everyone has priorities.
Rejecting biological materialism to the extent that
you no longer care if others find you attractive
is a lot like a country
that abhors capitalism to such a degree that they're
willing to live a minimalist existence
which may or may not include squalor and starvation,
in order for civilization to prosper in other ways.

Looking at the row of beautiful young girls in chairs
needlessly getting their cake faces put on,
as they gaze into handheld mirrors which reflect
an ugliness only visible to them....
it's clear they've bought into all the
billions of dollars of marketing ads and propaganda,
which has infiltrated their minds and

brainwashed them into thinking they need to
purchase more and more of these products
in order to be what they already were before
they even spent a dollar.
They're actually paying someone to
make them look more insecure and less attractive,
which is how they appear to anyone with the X-Ray eyes.
In their defense,
they may not desire someone focused enough to
see through the walls of superficiality they've constructed.

Whenever I walk by a young girl being made-up in the mall,
I feel the urge to walk up to her,
interrupt the operation and coax her out of the chair,

"You don't need that makeup. Don't waste your money. You're already prettier than the disgusting alien creature that's applying that stuff to your face. That make-up artist isn't the pied piper, and these rats can't show you where it's at."

Being on top of a girl that I once thought was
irresistible in a filtered photo and
now watching the mascara run
down from her fake eyelashes, and
the foundation melting into a mess of a face unmasked,
far from beauty and sex appeal, I now only
can see a being of insecurity and
feel only pity for a sad person whose confidence was
revealed to be as counterfeit as
the world of pure profit and
less admirable than one with a total lack of it.

This all could have been avoided.

THE LOOKOUT MAN

Survival often requires maintaining an
us vs. them mentality.
There's always an us whether we choose to accept it or not
(is it even a choice we can consciously make?)
At a certain point I began to recognize there was
no longer an us
as I once understood it.

Disappointed,
My concept of us morphed into me,
and the them became everyone else.
Like the last legionnaire in an abandoned Algerian outpost,
I stood alone, surrounded by enemies on all sides.
Still, always on the lookout for us.

Traveling through the grooves of the most happening cities,
surveying the vast circuitry,
scanning the crowds for coded signals…
In even the extremest of circumstances,
each of us left to our own devices
seeks out our own kind.

SQUEEZED OUT

His heart sank to the floor
overwhelmed by forces he had no control over.
He couldn't do anything but lie there
feeling the equivalent of the atmospheric pressure of Venus
crushing the matter which propels whatever it is one perceives as spirit
while sulfuric acid burned away
what was left of the will to live.

One final dream was brief but flickered vividly,
beaming through the densest of clouds

THE FERRYMAN

If you want to explore the stars,
you have to join the corporation.
They're the only ones still interested in venturing into space.
Corporations tend to enter space for all the wrong reasons,
not to expand man's knowledge of the solar system or
form colonies to advance the chance of
our survival as a species
but to exploit these other worlds
as a means to make money here on earth.
There may have been a dreamer behind
the schemers somewhere,
a billionaire stuck in traffic, staring up at the sky
seeking greater meaning,
but the machine is the machine and
once you turn them on,
machines do what machines are capable of doing.
They head to the moon not for the breathtaking views
but to mine the surface, to strip it bare
selling whatever minerals or other natural resources
they can muster away from a dusty old crater,
first displayed, then auctioned to a high bidder.
They offer the only shuttle ride in town though.
For the curious dreamer and determined explorer,
the ticket to way out is
to weasel your way into
the inner workings of the corporation.
It's our everyday struggle to keep one foot
in place where it needs to be
with the other out of step
however slightly
striding toward something we can't quite
reach, always just beyond that rare mineral beach
where the moon ferryman lets us off.

Still as we dig, we'll never stop seeking.

BREAKING THE CYCLE

Sometimes when I'm driving down a stretch of road,
the timing will be such
that I hit each and every red light.
The power behind the lights
seems to be conditioning us so that
in order to make the lights,
one must travel at a certain speed...
a speed too caterpillar-like to be meant for our kind.
I realize the only way to break the cycle
is to run one of the red lights in the series.
Once in awhile you have to force your way out of a rut
and into the green. When the system is electronically rigged,
it's time to tune out.
We've got to stay moving.
Like plants we are biologically driven to grow.
Through the light, Go!

THE INVOLVED

Conservatives always say "McCarthy was right!" and
I'm like "Yeah!
Eugene McCarthy was right!"
The Vietnam War was a shitshow and
an unnecessary waste of human lives.
Not even counting the money,
it's hard to believe that anyone believed it
was worth even one American's dead body
to enter the conflict in the first place.
It had nothing to do with us.
We had interests closer to home to be more
concerned with,
interests we've neglected ever since
our involvement,
everywhere.

DILATION

While exiting the coffee shop I spotted a
clean young girl of unwitting opposition,
instantly, a maxed out attraction.
She had the dangerous kind of smile that could potentially
erase the hate from my heart.
I hurried past her before it could affect me.
Have to keep moving...
Discipline in these matters is crucial.
In the span of a few seconds my mind cycled through
an entire relationship with her
from the first awkward conversation
through courtship
holding hands at the zoo
while watching otters frolic near the railing
waiting to be fed by clueless guests,
extended hangouts leading to
depraved sexual encounters,
post orgasm depression and pregnancy anxiety,
hundreds of meals eaten together
trivial arguments accompany
lingering doubts and underlying concerns as
months and months go by
romance fades to bitter shades
while trust is laid to rest
I could think of reasons to stay, but
they could not outweigh whatever is left
separated.
Thankfully the hatred returned.
Have to keep moving, quickly toward something
away from something else
Time slows down for a fast moving object
There is so much to do, and
every fraction of a second counts.
I hurried past her while experiencing a compact version of her love
which she would never be remotely aware the extent of.

THE PROJECTED

I conveyed in very abstract terms to her
the qualities and attributes I was seeking in companions
and spoke of the void
which would be filled by such ideal pairings
a thousand times over.
Disappointed that what I seemed to be after
did not relate to a specific girl
did not relate to her exclusively
but was perceived a mere myriad of holographic images
that in her mind could be projected upon almost anyone
who might entertain them,
she seemed dejected.

"It sounds like you're looking for something, not someone"

That's what I've tried to convince myself.

"So are you like, looking for something serious?"

On some level, we're all desperately searching for
someone and something.
I'm more serious about who the "ones" are
than what the "thing" is.

WAITING FOR THE TRAM

A lone holdout navigates garbage filled streets,
the foreign owned mini mart on the corner,
with lines of disheveled people purchasing
fruitless scratch lottery tickets.
Witness the Pavlovian salivation over market tested,
calculated snack attacks.

Further down the road,
crowded swap meets with hordes of riff raff
exchanging tokens for tiny jars of expired baby food…
Obese extended families of twelve
sauntering through outlet stores
gleefully purchasing cheap Chinese junk,
ugly silver painted trinkets and mindless gadgetry
labored in sweatshops
by poisoned air breathing peasants.
Nearby neighborhoods,
long ago bulldozed mid-century modern marvels,
their gutted shells replaced
with corner cut makeshift stucco huts
gated illusions from violent shantytowns
where unsupervised stray offspring spend their days
wilding in urban loin cloths strewn from
red tag thrift store clothing
followed by barely grown subhumans
mindlessly humping each other-

procreating,
procreating,
swamping
transforming,
demoralizing...

Demoralized, the finally aware remnants
flee to far off enclaves
rumored to exist,
dreaming not just of monorails on the moon or
hourly trams running through the icy caverns of Barsoom
but those which track to a future,
that makes room for their own.

EMOTIONAL THRILL POTIONS

A curious young girl asked me why certain men
seemed to prefer young women.
Besides the obvious attraction to increased fertility,
there is an element of vampirism.
As men grow older, they long to regain their
youth and innocence,
a sense of zest for life,
optimism,
a hope for the future,
which has long since faded into the rearview mirror,
even while those around them may not even notice.
A young woman has an abundance of all this.
By involving himself with a young chick,
the vampirist drains a bit of her innocence and
drinks it like an emotional thrill potion,
replenishing a bit of the vitality and youthful energy
for an undefined period of time.
As the girl ages quickly,
the man may becomes less enchanted.

Having had his fix, he discards her and
from the first daydream seeks out another.
The girl leaves the situation distraught,
a tad of her innocence permanently lost.
She becomes more averse to the sunny disposition,
the outline of which
could once be traced on her face.

Yet she also gains experience and
a cunning that will serve her well.
With each such experience,
she herself undergoes a slow transformation
into a succubus...

If the older gentlemen invests too much of himself,
gambling to obtain a more complex experience of
unfulfilled teenage romantic love,
the youthful energy he gains from an affair with
a young chick will be offset
as the bulk of it seeps out of the cracks his broken heart.
Lost and gained, the creatures move on
in search of new blood and emotions old.

NEPTUNED OUT

The steady flow of makeshift
boats made its way to shore,
each vessel filled beyond its capacity
with sub-literate and impoverished passengers galore.
Some children were sacrificed on the voyage and
did not survive the journey.
Intentions irrelevant,
those arriving would be invaders
by any measure of their transformative effect
on the welcoming society.
In small numbers they would mildly dilute and mutate
into more friendly blended shapes,
but in large groups it would be the native population
whom would be forced to assimilate
to a new reality of backwardness,
increased rape, violence, and animal cruelty.

The boats kept coming though.
No one that could have
was willing to stop them.
Voices of those who found
the sea change in culture undesirable
were drowned out.

Now the babies are growing,
their numbers swelling day by day.
Time's not on our side.
Without the means to stem the tide,
we'll reluctantly find ourselves swimming away.

THE LAST LOIS LANE

Some guy had planted fruit trees in the middle of the street.
So now there were full grown trees blocking
huge portions of the road.
I couldn't believe this didn't seem to bother anyone, and
that no one was doing anything about it.
I woke up within that dream…you know one of those
perplexing moments when you wake from
sleeping in a dream and somehow think you're
not dreaming anymore since you woke up.

Suddenly I discovered I was covered in tattoos.
They were good tattoos from what I could judge and
apparently were placed there by some female friends.
I tried to figure out how they could have
done it while I was asleep.
Had I been drugged or something?
I tried to wash them off, only to
discover that they were permanent.
I then however, woke up again within the dream,
and the tattoos were gone.
Ah thank goodness it was only a dream, yet
I didn't realize I was still dreaming even then.

I was lounging around in some unknown airport,
in a heavily trafficked area near one of the exits.
A somewhat dirty, white German shepherd dog wandered
up to my chair and wanted to be petted.
I was nervous, because you never know if
strange dogs will just decide to bite the shit out of you.
Its owner seemed to be nowhere to be found, but finally a
white trash looking lady came by and claimed the animal.

As I'm sitting there, I'm watching an anime series on
a portable little gadget I apparently own.
The anime series is a fictitious older one
which is titled "The Last Lois Lane."

As the theme song is playing,
there's an older Asian man several seats away from me
singing along with the words, as if the tune is
something he's nostalgic for from his childhood.

However, he seems too old to be nostalgic for
an anime series that's maybe at the most a couple of decades old.
He would have been a full grown adult
at the time when it aired....
so I figured he must have watched it with his children, and
maybe he's reminiscing about the
time he used to spend with them.
I wish that I could remember the words to the song, but
I'm afraid it was all just gibberish.
Though maybe it was just in Japanese, and
I didn't recognize it since I don't speak the language.
I don't want to offend anyone.

PATHOLOGY

I'm not following any yellow brick road
that has a vagina at the end of it.
I know how that story ends.
Out pops a wizard who informs you
that you made the trip for nothing,
helps you only to realize that whatever happiness and
blissful fulfillment you were
hoping to find inside her,
in fact already exists within you
and could have been discovered exploring by yourself
this entire time.

Booby traps, dildoes and all though,
the path through to the fairer sex may be as
irresistible as it is treacherous, and
sometimes a journey a few miles on
the trail of tough toenails
is worthwhile for the assortment of
hen houses, twin trees and prismed shapes in drapes
you encounter along the way.

THE GOOD TIMING

When I was a child,
things in life would be good for a long while,
and then it would end(my goodness!)
As a young teenager,
things would end just as they were getting good,
or so my feeble mind wagered at the time.
In my young adulthood,
things tended to end as I thought
they were about to begin to get good.
Amidst the present tensions,
good things seem to end even before they begin
leaving little time to wonder
what might have been.
In the future then,
all things will begin to end.

MIRROR ON THE MOON

There's space to breathe on the moon,
space which acts as a filtration system.
It separates us from whom and what we hate
back on Earth.
Even if they want to, they just can't make it here.
Sometimes I stare out the window of
my humble lunar condo,
not much more than a small room.
I gaze upon the endless rocks and many craters outside.
There are no plants, no scurrying little animals,
no birds chirping and no trees, no changing leaves...
just a world that's dark, quiet and mostly empty,
but as many times as I've seen it,
it never looks bleak.

For the longest time, we reflexively
reached in our back pocket for
our ancestral heritage and embraced our history
but eventually discovered the image in the rearview mirror
was not reciprocated as it appeared.
The others in our Earthly homelands
no longer saw us as their own kind.
We finally had to accept that we'd adapted into
a new biological identity, and that
it was time to let go of what we could of the past,
establish new traditions and
cultivate new institutions.
The moon is our home now, and
becoming physically a part of it is our mission.

THE EMPTYING GLASS

From the immaculate innocence granted every single infant
to the energetic empty promise of the prepubescent,
gearing toward the angst ridden adolescent
with his curious penchant
for all things perverted,
marathon running through the whirlwind that is
the grueling world the adult lives
chasing dreamlike images that lie almost always
just off in the distance,
facing up to the beginning moments of
middle age with at best
hopefully some crowning achievement
or less a brief minute of redempt
before fading into the flickering finality
beneath the fluorescent.

BREAD OF THE REALM

The oil beckons
like a materialist mirage
in the asphalt.
Desperate seekers tread ahead
failing to notice the trail of blood

ASCENDING ORDER

Synchronized goose steps,
jackboots locked in search of kicks,
new grounds and
inhumane faces to stomp on.
Purveyors of radical trad fads
get a tad uneasy
as we go wild pushing through the boundaries
of genetic experiments, scaling the wall toward
heightened experiences of bionic sexuality
and cryonic longevity.

BATTLE OF RAVENNA RAVINE

An aluminum arrow whizzes by the head
making a sound not unlike the slurp of an articulated straw.
For a brief moment,
time glacialized in the mind
like the brain freeze
of two young lovers
sharing a vanilla malt at the old drug store.
A group of hoods barrel through the entrance,
flooding the scene with an abstract violence.
The 45 on the jukebox abruptly stops,
triggering an awakening from the flashback.
These bitter beginnings
offer renewed resolve for the attack.

LIKE, DEAD

Loudness emanates from the imposing orifices of
obnoxious people at every turn
hootin' and hollerin'
with illiterate pop music doing its thing to the
idiots all around me.
No one is immune,
every last one of them absolutely disgusting
unknowingly
unconscious of their taken space
for nothing,
thousands surround me...
Almost none of them could be accused of
being a carrier of the bright disease.
I can tell just by eyeballing,
see how easily they've fallen for the marketing
of gadgets, widgets, trinkets and
beads they didn't want or even need.
The smart kids are lost, brainwashed and scrambled
in the Ivy Tower
at their own great financial future cost...

I don't care about most of these people, and
if you know your groceries, neither do you.
The misguided,
the mindless consumers and their prized pets...
to call them even the shape of squares
would be too generous
with dimensions.

They're humans all right, absorbed in garbage unlike
anything the Western world has ever known.
Disengaged, my body walks among their kind,
because I know I can't remove them on my own,
and there's no way out flying saucer
to get us home.

About the Author

Named after the main character in a sleazy 1970's romance novel, (*The Flame and the Flower*,) Brandon Adamson is a writer and artist, who currently resides in Phoenix Arizona. He has been writing since 1995, and his work has appeared in many magazines, blogs and literary journals over the years.

www.brandonadamson.com